DUDLEY SCHOOLS
LIBRARY SERVICE

KU-113-056

Schools Library and Information Services

S00000748324

caring for us

I am a Nurse

Deborah Chancellor

Photography by Chris Fairclough

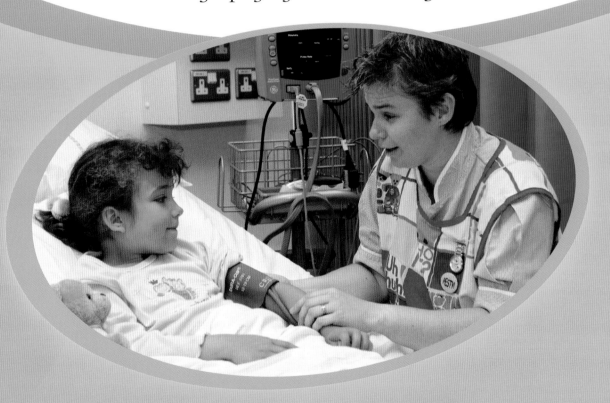

W

FRANKLIN WATTS
LONDON • SYDNEY

First published in 2010
by Franklin Watts
338 Euston Road
London NW1 3BH

Franklin Watts Australia
Level 17/207 Kent Street
Sydney, NSW 2000

Copyright © Franklin Watts 2010

All rights reserved.

Series editor: Jeremy Smith
Art director: Jonathan Hair
Design: Elaine Wilkinson
Photography: Chris Fairclough

Every attempt has been made to clear copyright.
Should there be any inadvertent omission please
apply to the publisher for rectification.

Thanks to Claire, Susan, Stephanie, Lisa, Geraldine and the
Children's Services staff at Addenbrooke's Hospital, Cambridge.

Dewey classification: 610.7'3069

ISBN 978 0 7496 9516 3

Printed in China

Franklin Watts is a division of Hachette Children's Books,
an Hachette UK company.
www.hachette.co.uk

Contents

Words in **bold** are in the glossary on page 24.

My job

I am a nurse.
I help people who
are sick or hurt
to get well again.

What do you think?

When
might people
go to see
a nurse?

4

I work in a **hospital** called Addenbrooke's,
in the city of Cambridge.

At the hospital

There are lots of different **wards** in my hospital.
I work on one of the children's wards.

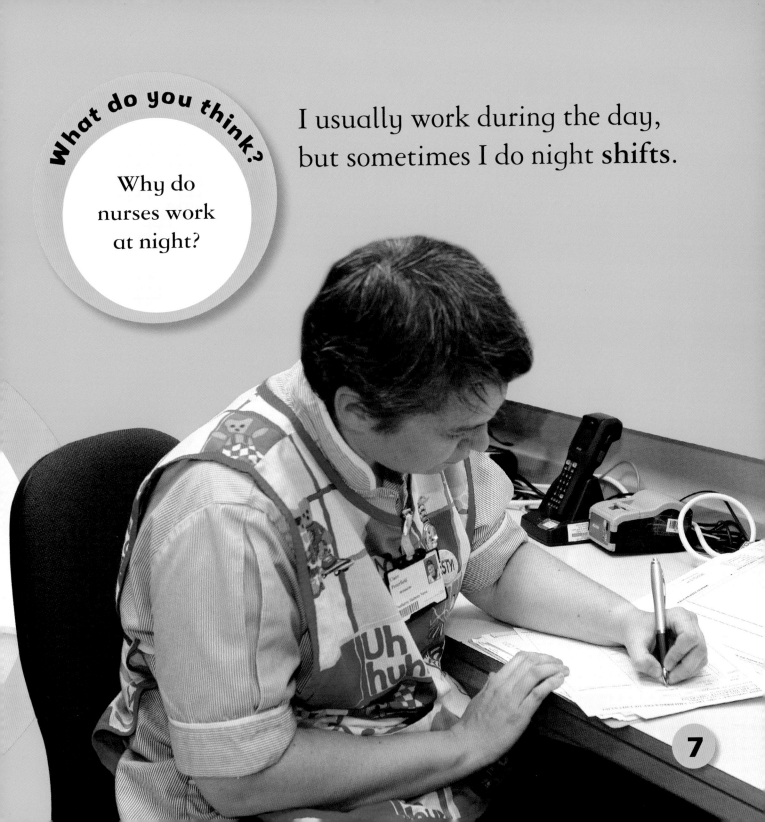

What do you think?

Why do nurses work at night?

I usually work during the day, but sometimes I do night **shifts**.

7

Children's ward

Children come to my ward for **treatment**, or for an **operation** that they need to have.

Do you know?
There are lots of different jobs in hospitals. Can you name some?

I work with a team of nurses on the ward.
The nurse in charge is called the senior sister.

9

New patients

When a new **patient** arrives at the ward,
I welcome them and show them around.

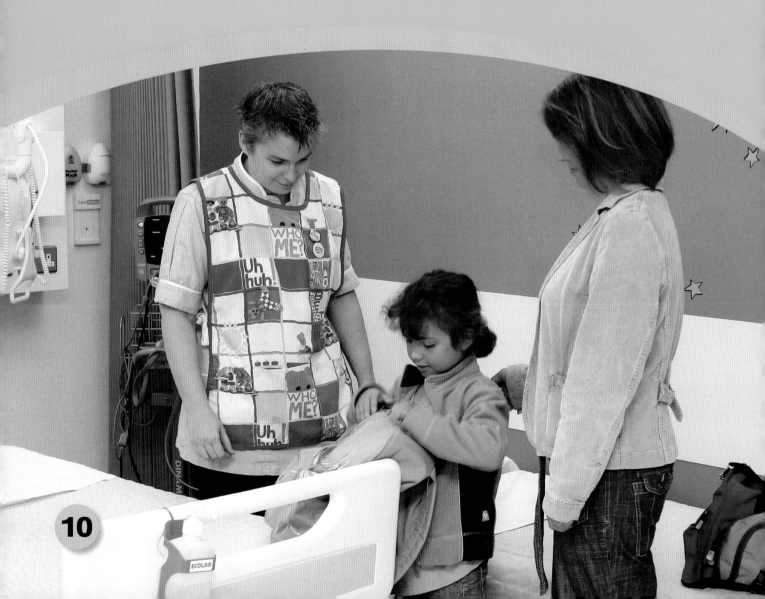

Some children just come for the day, and others stay for longer. Parents can stay with their children overnight.

What do you think?

How might new patients feel when they arrive in hospital?

11

Play time

Children can play in hospital. **Play specialists** help patients to relax and have fun.

12

What games could children play in hospital?

Playing can help children understand the treatment they are going to have.

13

Helping people

Every day, I take my patients' temperature, and feel their wrist to check their **pulse**.

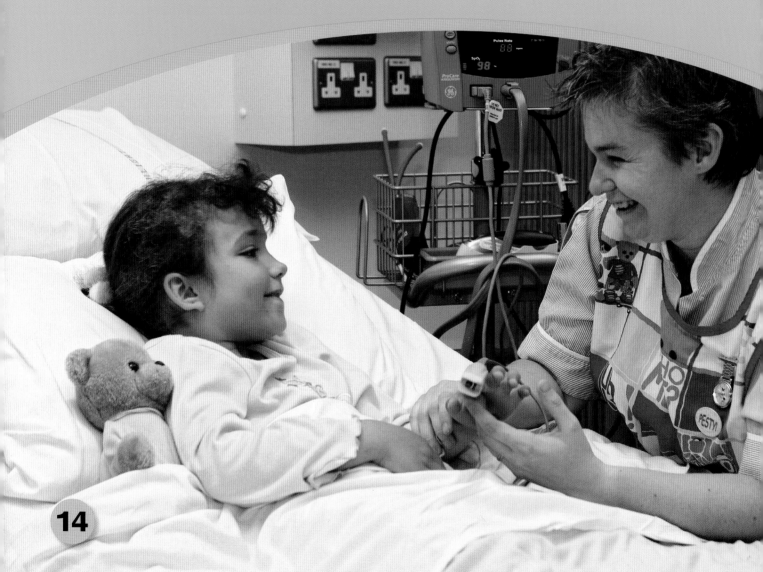

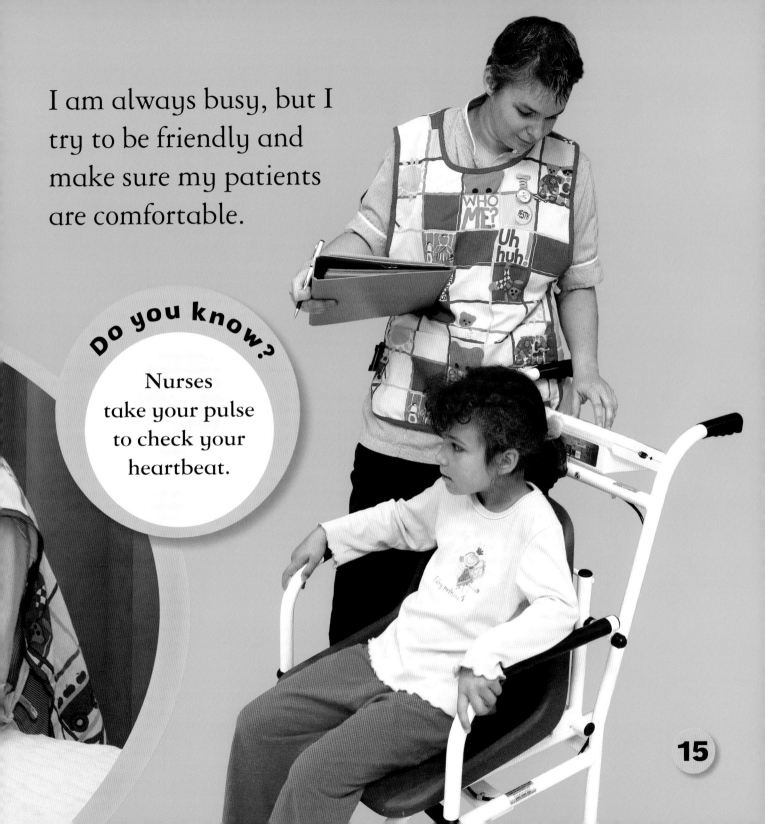

I am always busy, but I try to be friendly and make sure my patients are comfortable.

Do you know?

Nurses take your pulse to check your heartbeat.

15

Keeping well

I use a **syringe** to measure the right amount of medicine for my patients.

16

I always wash my hands when I finish doing something, so I don't pass on **germs**.

Do you know?
Hospitals are kept very clean so that germs don't spread.

17

In a meeting

Every day, I have meetings with other members of staff. We talk about what our patients need.

Each patient has a patient notes file,
with medical information inside.

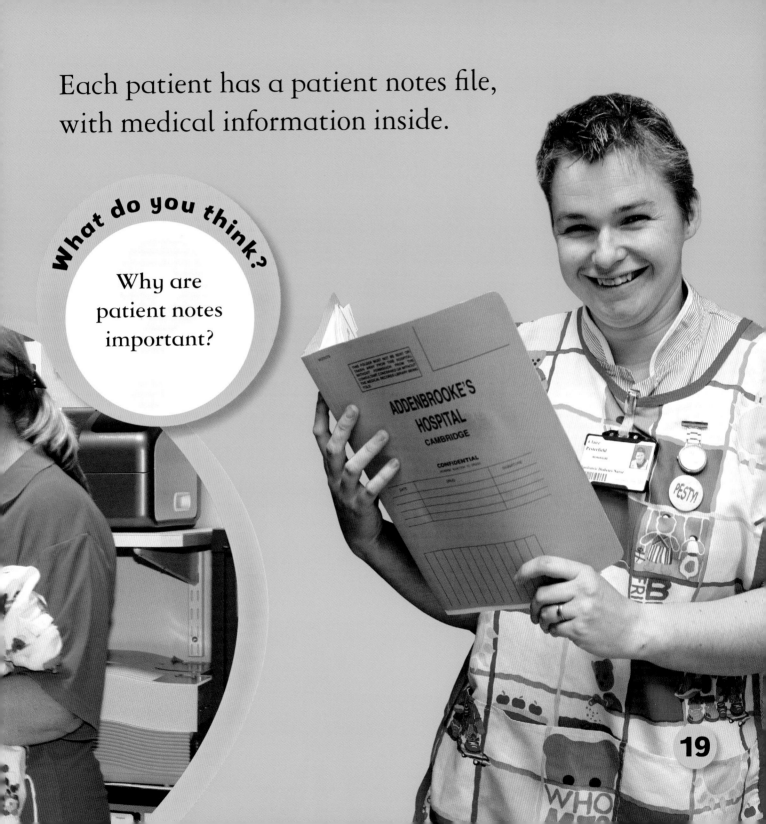

What do you think?

Why are
patient notes
important?

ADDENBROOKE'S
HOSPITAL
CAMBRIDGE

CONFIDENTIAL

Going home

When children are ready to leave hospital, I talk to them about the care they will need at home.

What do you think?

Would you like to be a nurse? Why?

At the end of my shift, it's time for me to leave. I'll be back again tomorrow!

Take care

Have fun, but take care when you play, so you don't get hurt and have to go to hospital. Always wear a helmet when you ride a bike, for example.

Look after your body, and eat the right kind of food, so you stay fit and well.

Do you know?

You need to eat at least five portions of fruit and vegetables a day.

Glossary

germs tiny living things that can make you ill

hospital a place where sick or injured people are looked after

operation something done to a patient's body to remove or mend a part of it

patient a person who is being treated in a hospital

play specialist an expert in how children play

pulse the speed that your heart beats

shift the hours a person is at work

syringe a piece of equipment with a tube for measuring medicine

treatment medical care

ward a room for patients in a hospital

Index